Backyard Birds

Matea Dickey

WestBow Press books may be ordered through booksellers or by contacting:

WestBow Press
A Division of Thomas Nelson & Zondervan
1663 Liberty Drive
Bloomington, IN 47403
www.westbowpress.com
1 (866) 928-1240

ISBN: 978-1-9736-7067-4 (sc)
ISBN: 978-1-9736-7068-1 (e)

Library of Congress Control Number: 2019911720

Print information available on the last page.

WestBow Press rev. date: 12/30/2019

WESTBOW
PRESS®
A DIVISION OF THOMAS NELSON
& ZONDERVAN

Acknowledgement

I would like to thank my mom for inspiring me to put this project together and a local artist who guided me to paint the paintings.

Backyard Birds

Words and pictures by
Matea Dickey

One sunny day, Ava wanted to go in her backyard. She put on her shoes and walked outside. As soon as she stepped out, She heard a tweeting sound and looked up.

There was a Blue Jay high in the tree top looking down at her. She said, "What a colorful blue bird"!

The Blue Jay flew to a tree on the other side of the yard. Ava said, "Wait up"!

She walked to the bush and saw the Blue Jay eating some berries.

Ava turned her head and observed a Red Robin pulling a worm out of the ground.

A Chickadee Bird flew over her head to a little tree behind her.

In the distance she saw a tree full of Cedar Waxwings.

There are birds all around us, even in our backyard!

Printed in the United States
By Bookmasters